super green
smoothies

super green
smoothies

60 delicious recipes for weight loss, energy and vitality

SALLY OBERMEDER
& MAHA KORAIEM

ALLEN&UNWIN
SYDNEY · MELBOURNE · AUCKLAND · LONDON

First published as an ebook in 2014 by Swiish Pty Ltd

This edition published in 2015

Allen & Unwin
83 Alexander Street
Crows Nest NSW 2065
Australia
Phone: (61 2) 8425 0100
Email: info@allenandunwin.com
Web: www.allenandunwin.com

Cataloguing-in-Publication details are available from the
National Library of Australia
www.trove.nla.gov.au

ISBN 978 1 76011 371 1

Design by transformer.com.au, Sydney
Set in 10/14 pt PMN Caecilia by transformer.com.au, Sydney

Colour reproduction by Splitting Image Colour Studio Pty Ltd, Clayton, Victoria

Printed and bound in China by Hang Tai Printing Company Ltd

20 19 18 17 16 15 14 13 12 11 10

'I am a big believer in clean living. Green smoothies are an incredible way to increase wellness, weight loss and energy. You'll find Sally's recipes help you do just that. One of her smoothies every day will give you a shot of good health. They're quick and easy to make plus they taste delicious. *Super Green Smoothies* is bound to become your daily go-to guide and your best friend in the kitchen.'

James Duigan,
celebrity trainer, whose clients include Elle Macpherson, Rosie Huntington-Whiteley and Lara Stone; Creator of Bodyism; and author of the bestselling *Clean & Lean Diet*

contents

how it all began

I live an extremely busy, action-packed, fulfilling yet exhausting life. I love all aspects of it. Being the mother of a gorgeous two-year-old is just like the cliché—the most challenging but rewarding experience. I love being married to my husband (despite him saying I shop too much).

I am blessed to have a TV job that I am passionate about, and fortunate enough to work with a hilarious, insanely interesting and intelligent bunch who are also my friends.

My blog, swiish.com.au, is also a big part of my life: I get to work on a range of lifestyle topics on a daily basis with my sister Maha—she is not only my very best friend but also the world's most amazing sister. We bicker and banter like everyone, but at the end of the day we wouldn't change a thing.

Throw into the mix family, friends, exercise and social commitments, and you get a life jam-packed like a tin of sardines, but I wouldn't change it for anything! I feel I'm at my best and happiest when there's a whole heap of things on my plate and I'm juggling it all. That said, there are times when the juggling can get too much. It can become draining and exhausting, but I don't want to give up a thing. The most important thing to me, however, is that my health does not suffer because of it. And so enter the humble smoothie.

A bit of background. I was diagnosed with Stage 3 breast cancer in late 2011, the day before giving birth to my daughter, Annabelle. The cancer was rare and extremely aggressive. What followed was a torturous year of chemotherapy, radiation, a double mastectomy and numerous other surgeries. I was fortunate to be given the all-clear in late 2012. While I no longer had cancer, I was now faced with another challenge—rebuilding my body, which had been annihilated by the treatment as well as affected by the usual strains and exhaustion that most women face during their first year of motherhood.

I decided that 2013 was my year to get back to 'me'. I wanted to regain my health, and also lose the baby weight and the extra 15 kilos I put on during chemotherapy. As much as I wish I had a supermodel's genes and access to a personal chef, I don't. I needed to do something that would fit in with my family and work commitments. I wanted good health, vitality, energy and overall wellness but not at the expense of altering my entire lifestyle. I knew that if it was too hard, or too extreme, chances were I wouldn't be able to sustain it.

I had heard about green smoothies and decided I needed to try them. Little did I know that such a small change in my diet could have such dramatic results. The kilos came off more easily than I ever expected. My skin glowed, my hair and nails got stronger and my energy levels went through the roof. I felt light, lean, strong, healthy and happy.

I genuinely felt, and continue to feel, the best I have in a long time (even compared to before I had cancer). Through one simple change, I am motivated to lead a healthier life. And because I know I'm looking after myself, I'm happier.

Over the last year a *lot* of people have been saying they're shocked by how well and slim I look. When I explain how wonderful I feel, they're even more surprised. Everyone asks the same question: 'What are you doing?'

Which brings me to this book. Instead of writing all my recipes on sticky notes, I decided that this was a better way to share what I know. And since Maha also adopted a smoothie lifestyle with similar results to me, we worked on creating new recipes together.

We genuinely feel that everyone can achieve improved wellness and health through this one simple daily change.

Every day we are hounded with new information on health. The fads are constantly changing, the messages about what's healthy and what's not are contradictory, and it can sometimes feel overwhelming and hard to know what to do. Drinking healthy smoothies is an easy adaptation for even the busiest person, and the benefits are many—weight loss, increased energy, clearer skin, and improved digestion and immunity, to name just a few.

Being healthy should be enjoyable. Green smoothies are simple and affordable and taste great. I truly hope this book inspires you to go green, get lean and love a smoothie as much as I do!

Love Sally x

the
smoothie
lifestyle

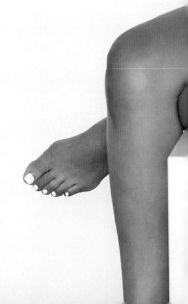

1
getting
organised

before you begin

I'll try to address as many important things as I can upfront, in order to make your routine of a daily green smoothie as easy as possible. Eventually, though, you'll just have to dive right in and start making them. I promise you'll look and feel better for it.

Blending versus juicing

I'm often asked whether blending is better than juicing, and my answer is always the same—they're both equally important for your body. Both give your body nutrients in an easier, more efficient way than eating all those vegies and fruits on their own. (Can you really eat spinach, kale, broccoli, celery, avocado, lemon and banana in one sitting? I know I can't!) They're also quick and easy to make, and taste delicious.

The difference between juicing and blending is that juicing removes the fibre in vegies and fruit that our bodies aren't able to digest easily, so you just get the nutrients. Blending, on the other hand, breaks the fibre down in a way that the body can digest it more easily. So you get the benefit of the fibre, which is good for your digestive tract, and the fibre also means you end up feeling full for longer.

There's been a lot of talk lately about cold-pressed juices, which are basically juices extracted from fruit and vegies by crushing and pressing. Because these processes don't generate as much heat as blending does, the nutrients remain predominantly intact. So while juicing is fine, I think blending is superior as you're consuming the whole vegetable or fruit.

Blending not only gives you nutrients and fibre but also the opportunity to add extras such as protein, good fats and oils, and superfoods such as chia seeds, maca powder, bee pollen and spirulina. All of these added extras give you the chance to boost your vitamin and mineral intake, which is great for lean muscle creation, increased energy, improved digestion, glowing skin, hair and nails, and improved immunity. Your body also benefits from all the nutrients in the flesh and skin of the produce: in most of my smoothie recipes, you will blend these as well.

Equipment

Right … so you need a blender. Both Maha and I have a commercial-quality blender and for us, this was the best choice. It is definitely an investment buy, but if you're committed to making a lifestyle change and having a smoothie every day then, in my view, it's 100 per cent worth it. Because my blender is so powerful, I can make a smoothie in less than two minutes. It blends ice and frozen fruits and vegies with ease. It also does other cool things like make ice-cream and soup (and heat it up), but truthfully I don't use it for any of those things. I just wanted a blender that could handle whole ingredients and save me time chopping.

Of course, not everyone wants to—or is in fact able to—fork out for one of these. And that's totally OK. You can still make great, healthy smoothies with a normal everyday blender that you can buy at a department or discount store. You just have to adjust the way you blend, and it might take a little longer to get the right consistency for your smoothie (for more information, see page 18).

TIP: When people ask me if it's worth the investment for a professional blender, I say that if you already own a blender of any kind, first use that and see how committed you are to making smoothies. If it turns out that you love smoothies and are making them regularly, you can always upgrade. I just encourage you to start today with what you have to hand.

Smoothie tips for beginners

When you're creating your own smoothie recipe, I recommend aiming for 60 per cent vegies and 40 per cent fruit. Over time, you can increase this to 70 per cent vegies and 30 per cent fruit, which is what I do. You'll find that different fruits have different levels of sweetness, so you can tweak your recipes accordingly. For example, dates and frozen bananas are very sweet, whereas apples don't give you the same hit of sweetness. In this book, we've created different sections to allow for your smoothie 'evolution'—beginning with some simple recipes and working right up to 100 per cent vegie smoothies.

Mix your greens up! Although I love spinach and kale, it's important to switch greens on a regular basis. Why? Well, almost all leafy Brassicas—spinach, silverbeet (Swiss chard) and rocket (arugula)—contain small amounts of what are known as alkaloids. If you consume the same green for weeks on end, and don't rotate them, then the alkaloids can build up in your body and you will develop the symptoms of alkaloid poisoning. These can include nausea, cold sweats, tingling in the fingers and headaches. Admittedly, you'd need to consume quite a lot to get alkaloid poisoning but it can happen, so I want to flag it. Besides, rotating your greens will provide you with added nutritional benefits. Try rotating varieties of lettuce with bok choy, rocket (arugula), radicchio, sprouts or endive.

Drink your smoothie straightaway. If you have some left over, store it in an airtight container or mason jar and pop it in the fridge, where it will keep for 24 hours. If you know you won't be able to finish the smoothie in that time, freeze it. You can always pop it back into your blender a couple of days later, along with some fresh ice and fresh herbs or lemon juice for extra zing.

I believe that frozen ingredients are best for a few reasons. First, colder smoothies generally taste better. Second, making the smoothie is quicker and easier—if you have prepared your ingredients by peeling (for example, avocado and other tough-skinned fruits and vegetables) and chopping them before you freeze them, they're right there, prepped and ready to go. Finally, you can cut down on food wastage—whenever you have fresh fruit, vegies or herbs in your fridge that are on the verge of becoming overripe or soft, or going off, you can freeze them for your smoothies instead of tossing them out. Gotta love that!

Sometimes, when you experiment with new vegie and fruit combos, you will make a smoothie that just doesn't taste great. It happens. Instead of throwing it out, grab an ice-cube tray, pour in your smoothie and freeze. You can throw a few cubes into a sweeter-tasting smoothie on another day. Freezing smoothies into ice cubes is also a good idea when you've made a batch that's too big. No wastage!

fresh and frozen

I'm often asked about which fruit and vegies you can or can't freeze to use in smoothies. The reality is that you can make every smoothie with fresh or frozen ingredients, or a combination of the two.

I tend to use frozen ingredients because I like to be organised and have every-thing in my freezer prepared, labelled and ready to go.

It's fine to use fresh ingredients, but you'll need to add a bunch of ice cubes to make it icy because that generally makes it taste best. But know that when you do this, you'll also be diluting the consistency of the smoothie and therefore the intensity of the flavour—another reason why I prefer frozen ingredients.

Ingredients to always have in your freezer

Avocado: Remove the skin and seed, then freeze into halves.

Banana: Peel it then, if you don't have a commercial-grade blender, slice it up before freezing.

Berries: I always use frozen berries, as they're cheaper and I can have them on hand, regardless of the season. Freeze in 70 g (2½ oz/½ cup) servings.

Broccoli: Chop it into smaller florets.

Brussels sprouts: Halve these before freezing.

Celery: Use whole stalks, with the leaves attached, but chop them before freezing.

Cucumber: Chop into halves.

Endive: Freeze into 25 g (1 oz/1 cup) servings.

Grapes: I freeze both red and green.

Green beans: Freeze into 60 g (2¼ oz/½ cup) servings.

Herbs: Use mint, basil and parsley, and freeze them in bunches.

Kale: Freeze into 50 g (1¾ oz/2 cups) servings.

Kiwi fruit: Peel and halve.

Lemons: Peel and halve.

Limes: Leave peel on and quarter.

Lettuce: Freeze into 40 g (1½ oz/1 cup) servings.

Mango: I buy frozen mango from my local fruit store and keep it year round. If you're using fresh mango, peel and remove the stone.

Passionfruit: Scoop out the pulp and seeds before freezing them.

Pineapple: If you can't get your hands on a fresh pineapple, use tinned. Drain the juice, then rinse before freezing.

Rocket (arugula): Freeze into 20 g (¾ oz/1 cup) servings.

Snow peas: Freeze into 50 g (2 oz/½ cup) servings.

Spinach: Freeze into 45 g (1½ oz/1 cup) servings.

Stone fruits: Freeze these only once they're ripe. Remove the stone before chopping.

Tomatoes: Chop these first.

Watermelon: Freeze into 175 g (6 oz/1 cup) servings.

fridge and pantry

There are a few items I like to keep on hand in my fridge and pantry that give smoothies an added boost. By no means do you have to get all of these. I just like to mix up my smoothies for both nutrition and taste.

Maybe start with a few and see how you go

Cacao: You can use both powder and nibs.

Coconut water: I like to use the water from a fresh coconut. If I can't get that I'll use a carton variety (see also page 13).

Flavour boosters: Try vanilla extract and shredded coconut.

Green supplement powders: Generally available from health food and vitamin shops, these are a blend of nutrient-dense greens, fibre, fruits, vegies, vitamins, minerals and antioxidants.

Milk: Cow's milk, almond milk, rice milk, coconut milk, oat milk, soy milk and quinoa milk.

Nut butter: Almond butter, cashew butter and peanut butter.

Nut meal: Almond meal, hazelnut meal and flaxseed (linseed) meal.

Nuts and seeds: Raw almonds, Brazil nuts, walnuts, macadamias and pumpkin seeds.

Oils: Coconut oil, flaxseed (linseed) oil and hemp oil.

Protein powder: Adding protein powder to smoothies is a quick and efficient way to add protein, which helps you feel full for longer. If I am having my smoothie post-workout, I generally add protein powder but there are no hard and fast rules. Flavour-wise my preferences are vanilla, banana and coffee, but if chocolate or berry is more your thing, then just follow your taste buds. It's a great idea to keep a few flavours on rotation in the pantry.

Spices: Ginger, cinnamon, turmeric, allspice and nutmeg.

Sugar-free sweeteners: Stevia and rice malt syrup.

Superfoods: Goji berries, bee pollen, chia seeds, maca powder, spirulina, liquid chlorophyll and probiotic powder. Superfoods are called 'super' because they really give your body a mega-boost of benefits, including aiding digestion, ramping up energy levels, increasing immunity and improving joint health.

Sweeteners: Honey, agave syrup and dates.

Holy Caca

CONTENTS
Fat Flush

food swaps

As you go through the recipes in the book you'll find that you may not have a certain ingredient on hand, or you love a particular recipe but want to try mixing things up a little. Go for it—the world is your smoothie!

Some swaps that work well

Milk: Alternate between full-fat, skim, soy, almond, rice, oat, quinoa or coconut milk—whatever you like. When I refer to coconut milk, I mean carton coconut milk, such as Coco Quench, not tinned coconut milk. The difference is the fat and kilojoule (calorie) content, with the carton variety being much lower. Coco Quench is a blend of organic coconut and rice milk and it tastes great. If you're going to use the tinned variety, opt for 'light' or, alternatively, go 50/50: half coconut milk, half water. If you want to go milk-free you can swap it with water.

Cacao powder: Swap cacao powder with cacao nibs.

Greens: If you don't have a particular green on hand—for example, silverbeet (Swiss chard), endive or radicchio—then you can instead use whatever you do have, such as cos lettuce, spinach, etc.

Lemons: Use either lemons or limes, whichever is in season and readily available.

Oils: I tend to use a lot of coconut oil due to its many health benefits—improved cholesterol and increased metabolism, plus it's also good for hair and skin—but if you don't have any in stock, you can use flaxseed (linseed) oil, hemp oil, rice bran oil, avocado oil, macadamia oil, pumpkin seed oil or walnut oil instead.

Protein powder: Use whatever variety suits you best—pea, whey, kelp, brown rice or casein. If you like you can also add a raw egg instead. I know it's not for everyone, but I love it.

Sweeteners: Use agave syrup or honey. You can also use dates if you prefer. If you are going sugar-free, opt for rice malt syrup or stevia.

Vanilla: Swap vanilla pods with vanilla extract or vanilla sugar.

Water: Switch coconut water and plain water.

Serving sizes

Our recipes serve either one or two. One serve is 500 ml (17 fl oz) or 2 cups. Two serves is 1 litre (35 fl oz) or 4 cups. I generally make enough for two serves: I have up to 750 ml (26 fl oz/3 cups) for breakfast and the rest as an afternoon snack. This is just my preference, but as always you should do what suits you best.

Breakfast, lunch or dinner?

Personally, I have my smoothie as a breakfast replacement because that's when I'm generally doing a million things and trying to rush out the door. For me, it means that I know I've had a massive kick-start of vegies, fruit, protein and superfood. So no matter what else happens that day, I know I've had a full day's worth of nutrients and vitamins. Any extra fruit and vegies I have after that is really just a bonus. I also find it gives me a massive morning buzz without caffeine. I feel good knowing that I've started my day right, and it makes me happy to know I'm looking after myself.

I have my second smoothie in the afternoon when things are hectic and I'm most susceptible to eating anything with fat or sugar, or both. The smoothie tastes great, it fills me up and it kills any cravings for processed food.

. . . .

TIP: So when should you have your smoothie? What are the rules? There are none. You can have yours whenever you want.

. . . .

If you prefer to replace your lunch or dinner with a smoothie, go right ahead. I prefer to sit down to a meal at night, but I have friends who don't and the night-time smoothie works better for them.

It's all about you and your lifestyle. You might not want a smoothie as a meal replacement. Fine. In that case simply have a smaller quantity with your meal.

Do what's right for you. As long as you're consuming a smoothie, it doesn't really matter whether it's 7 a.m. or 7 p.m. Your body will thank you.

Colour me happy

I try to eat a variety of vegies and fruits, so you'll see these smoothies in a few different colours. There's green, red, white, yellow, orange and brown. My aim is to give myself, and you, the maximum range of health benefits, and by eating the largest mix of fruit and vegies you possibly can, that's what you get.

The smoothies are predominantly based on green vegetables but I've also included a few of my favourite recipes that use beetroot, cauliflower, pumpkin and even radishes. The best diets are those that incorporate a mix of all the good stuff.

To help you pinpoint specific needs, such as weight loss, increased energy or improved digestion, I've put together a quick guide to let you know which smoothie recipes would be best. This guide can be found on page 166, but see also the guide to benefits provided with each recipe.

2

frequently asked questions

Why do you have smoothies?

Well, having a smoothie a day is one of the easiest, simplest changes I made to my diet, and what I gained in return was weight loss, more energy, clearer skin, shinier hair, better sleep, improved digestion and immunity, and a whole lot of nutrients. I also found it removed my desire for sugar and processed foods. There is no way I could sit down and eat this many greens in one go.

What equipment do I need to make smoothies?

All you need to make delicious smoothies are a sharp knife, a vegetable peeler, a chopping board and a blender.

Do I need to buy an expensive blender?

A blender is a great kitchen essential that can be used for many different purposes—soups, dips, etc.—so it is a good investment buy. However, you don't need to spend a heap of money to make great smoothies.

If you already have a blender, try it out and see how you go using it to make smoothies. You might need to adjust your ingredients slightly to get the right consistency. I suggest using a little more liquid and blending your greens and liquid first before adding the remaining ingredients. You may also need to add your ingredients gradually so that you don't overpower the motor of the blender, or add a little more liquid to achieve the right consistency, which may be necessary no what matter which type of blender you own.

The most important thing to do is just start. Remember, you can always upgrade later.

What is the difference between a juice and a smoothie?

Both juices and smoothies are great for your health. A juice contains only the liquid extracted from a fruit or vegetable, but although it contains very little dietary fibre it still contains vitamins and nutrients. A smoothie, on the other hand, has the lot—fibre, vitamins and nutrients.

Why are greens so important?

Green vegetables are high in vitamins and minerals, fibre, proteins, antioxidants, fat-burning compounds and healthy bacteria. They are also low in kilojoules (calories). Greens are also alkalising. What's the big deal about that? Well, alkalising your body refers to shifting the pH levels. Just as your your body needs to maintain a specific temperature, it must also maintain a pH which is slightly higher than 7. How do you alkalise your body? Eat more 'live' foods (such as fresh fruit and vegies) than acidic foods (such as meat, dairy and sugars). If you don't help your body maintain a slightly alkaline pH, then your body will try to deal with the excess acid for you. One way it does this is to create fat to neutralise the acid. Another thing the body must do is protect the arteries. The mechanism for this is cholesterol. If your blood is acidic, the body coats your arteries with cholesterol to protect them. On the upside, once you start to alkalise your body, all of these things rapidly change.

Greens also protect your body from illness, cleanse your kidneys and feed your brain.

They help your body maintain good health, clearer skin and shinier hair, build leaner muscles and ensure healthy digestion.

What can I put in a smoothie?

Follow the recipes. Maha and I have both made these and we know they taste great. You can, of course, create your own. If you do, we would love nothing more than for you to snap a pic and share it with us at swiish.com.au, or tag us @swiishbysallyo in your Instagram pic.

Doesn't it take a long time to make a smoothie?

Making a smoothie only takes a few minutes; preparation is the key. If you're always on the go, wash, chop and freeze your ingredients in advance (see also page 9). I keep my fruit and vegetable ingredients in resealable bags in the freezer, so I can use them at any time. To keep it easy, keep other ingredients such as spices, oils and nuts together so they're easy to grab and add.

I don't have time to make a smoothie every day. Can I make a bigger batch and refrigerate or freeze it?

Yes. Smoothies only last in the fridge for about 24 hours. After that, they lose some nutrients and won't taste as fresh. However, you can freeze smoothies. I freeze them in daily portions in air-tight containers or jars.

Defrost your smoothie in the fridge the night before you want to drink it, and it'll be thawed and ready to go by morning. You'll find it needs a little chlorophyll, lemon, lime or herbs to give it a fresh shot of zing and an added flavour boost.

What time of day is best to have a smoothie?

Whatever time you want. There is no 'best' time—you can have it for breakfast, lunch, dinner or a snack during the day.

Can I replace a meal with a smoothie?

Yes, you definitely can. I suggest you replace a meal where you tend to make poor choices or struggle to eat well. For me, during the week that meal is breakfast, simply because I'm trying to get dressed, ready and organised. Looking after my daughter, Annabelle, and getting her breakfast sorted used to mean buttery toast in the car for me.

Toast in itself isn't necessarily 'bad'; it's just that I wasn't giving my body the opportunity to absorb the greatest amount of nutrients it could. Unlike a Sunday breakfast where I generally eat eggs, avocado, spinach, mushroom and tomato with the toast, my midweek toast lacked protein, vitamin and minerals. So I wasn't starting my day with a bang.

It's different for everyone. I have a girlfriend who used to struggle to eat well at dinner. She confessed to wandering back and forth between the fridge and the pantry, aimlessly eating whatever she could get her hands on. For her, having a smoothie for dinner has been a game-changer. She's lost 8 kilos (17½ pounds), she's sleeping better and she's feeling the best she's felt in a long time.

Surely the smoothies taste awful. Spinach? Kale? Brussels sprouts? Really?

I think if I were to have a smoothie made up of only those three ingredients, I wouldn't like it very much. But add some fruit (bananas especially), superfoods and herbs, and then suddenly—woohoo! Deeeeelicious! Try them and you'll see.

You need to start gradually. Baby spinach leaves are the easiest vegetable to start with. Once you're accustomed to that, work up to kale, brussels sprouts and anything else you like. Also, as with all cooking, you need added flavour—that's where the fruit, nuts and oils come in. They give the smoothies so much flavour and taste. If you've got a sweet tooth you can also add your sweetener of choice—stevia is mine.

I don't like banana/mango/peach ... what can I replace it with?

If there's a fruit in one of the recipes that you don't like, then swap it with something you love. It's that easy. Can't eat banana? Switch it with dates, pineapple, mango or peaches. If you don't like pineapple, replace it with apple, pear or mango. Just keep the volume quantities the same—for example, swap 160 g (5½ oz/1 cup) of chopped pineapple with 185 g (6½ oz/1 cup) of chopped mango.

What sweeteners can I use?

You can sweeten your smoothies without using refined sugar. Here are some other, healthier options.

Low-kilojoule (low-calorie) sugar-free sweeteners: stevia and xylitol.

Low-GI sweeteners: coconut palm sugar, rice malt syrup and agave syrup.

Minimal processing: raw honey and date sugar.

I'm worried my smoothie will taste bitter from all the spinach and kale. How can I fix this?

The easiest way to reduce the bitterness is to add lemon or lime. A small squeeze should do the trick, but add more if it's needed.

Can green smoothies help with weight loss?

Absolutely! If you want to lose weight then green smoothies are such a good way to go about it. They can kick-start your digestion, reduce bad cholesterol, increase your energy, regulate and improve bowel movements, help you burn excess fat and decrease cravings for processed, sugary foods. Smoothies are packed with nutrients, vitamins and fibre. They're filling and they taste great, making it an easy lifestyle change to make.

You're not eating processed 'diet' food. Rather, you're consuming real food. Living food. Good food. Food that nourishes. Most of us have started a diet on Monday only to find ourselves binge-eating wildly like a half-starved animal by Wednesday. Because these smoothies taste great and are easy to make, it's a sustainable weight-loss method when combined with a balanced, healthy diet and exercise.

Can I use these smoothies to detox?

Vegetables are a great way to detox. The smoothies I would recommend are Watermelon Detox, Original Skinny and Fat Flush. As a general rule, if you're detoxing, you should remove dried fruits, additional sweeteners or dairy from recipes to get the best results.

How do I make my smoothie a smooth consistency without any leafy chunks?

If you don't have a high-speed blender, I suggest you blend liquids and any leafy vegies first until you achieve a juice-like consistency. Then gradually add the rest of your ingredients.

I'm getting a very thick, soupy consistency. Is this right?

This is a matter of personal preference. I don't mind my smoothies a little thicker. However, if you do, you can either blend for a little longer, or simply add a little extra liquid or a handful of ice cubes, then blend again until you achieve the desired consistency.

Should I peel my fruit and vegies, or leave them as is?

Apart from fruits and vegies with skin that is basically inedible—for example, banana, melon, mango, pineapple, avocado, etc.—I don't peel anything. So ingredients like cucumber, carrot, peach and apple go into the blender, skin and all. Just wash them well first.

Can I blend fruit seeds?

Aside from the obvious seeds you shouldn't blend—for example, stone fruit, avocado—seeds in fruits such as grapes, pomegranate, berries, passionfruit, watermelon and kiwi fruit are edible.

The seeds from apples and pears contain cyanide, but in such small amounts that if you do happen to have them, they shouldn't cause any major problems. I suggest you core all apples and pears prior to blending.

Citrus seeds have very small amounts of toxins, but they are fine to blend.

Papaya seeds, while not toxic, have a peppery flavour, which can overpower the smoothie, so I remove them.

My green smoothie turned brown. Is this normal?

Sometimes mixing fruits like strawberries or watermelon with green leafy vegetables will turn your smoothie brown. Don't worry—it will still taste good. But if you really don't like the colour, try adding dark berries to make it purple.

Isn't it too cold in winter to have smoothies?

I have my smoothies year round, but if you find it's too cold to drink smoothies in winter, you could try using fresh rather than frozen ingredients and drink your smoothie at room temperature. Recipes that include spices like cinnamon or ginger are perfect for winter, as they'll add a bit of warmth to your smoothie. Try White Out, Spiced Oatmeal & Nuts, Holy Cacao! or Papaya Pumpkin.

Help! My smoothie is warm.

This could be because you've used all fresh ingredients (as opposed to at least one frozen item) or you've let your blender run longer than it probably needs to. To fix this, add ice cubes and blend again, or pop your smoothie into the freezer for a short time to cool it down quickly.

To prevent this from happening again, as you're gradually adding your ingredients, add the next ingredient before the previous one is fully blended. This will keep the blending time to a minimum and the temperature down.

Can I make green smoothies for my kids?

Yes. We often try to sneak greens into our kids' meals and this is a great way for the little ones to get lots of tasty goodness in a glass. One of my girlfriends tells me her kids are big fans. The youngest one calls it *The Shrek* while the older one calls it *The Incredible Hulk* (after the movies of the same name). She's just glad they're loving spinach even if they don't realise it!

We've devoted a special recipe section to Mini-Me's in this book (see page 153). However, kids will love most of the other smoothies too. Just be sure to drop the protein powder when you're making anything for children.

Is a home-made smoothie healthier than buying one already made?

Generally, yes. When you make your own smoothie you can not only guarantee exactly what you are drinking but you can also control the portions and make it as healthy as you can. The smoothies you buy from an establishment or the store can be high in kilojoules (calories), sugar and fat, depending on which ingredients have been used. If you buy a pre-made smoothie, be sure to check the nutritional information to make sure it is healthy!

Why do you use almond milk in your smoothies?

Almond milk is a great source of protein; it's low in kilojoules (calories) and ticks the box for those who want dairy-free. You can also use rice, oat or quinoa milk if you like. If you prefer to go for dairy milk, then you can use full-fat or skim. If you like soy, that's OK too. It's totally up to you and your taste buds. Sometimes, if I want to keep it to just the fruit, vegies and superfoods, I use water in the recipes instead.

Can you suggest any low-sugar fruit options to replace banana?

We use bananas in our smoothies because they provide the perfect dense and creamy base. However, if you don't like bananas or prefer a low-sugar substitute, you can try using berries, pear, apple, peach, melons (rockmelon [cantaloupe], honeydew or watermelon), nectarines, pureed pumpkin, frozen peas or avocado instead. These will keep your smoothie tasty without the sugar spike.

I've created a recipe. Can I share it with you?

Please do! We would love to hear about, and see, any smoothies you make, whether they are from this book or ones that you've created yourself.

You can snap a pic and share it with us at **www.swiish.com.au** or tag us **@swiishbysallyo** in your Instagram pic.

We're here if you're tweeting **https://twitter.com/swiishbysallyo** Or find us on Facebook at **www.facebook.com/swiishbysallyobermeder**

recipes

3
start simple

MANGO MAGIC

DETOXIFYING • HAIR • SKIN • NAILS • ANTIOXIDANT-RICH • DIGESTION • ENERGY BOOSTER

UNDER 1256 kJ/300 Cal PER SERVE

90 g (3¼ oz/2 cups) baby spinach

1 frozen banana

185 g (6½ oz/1 cup) chopped mango

250 ml (9 fl oz/1 cup) vanilla almond milk
or soy milk

Place all the ingredients in a blender and blend until smooth.

SERVES 1

BANANARAMA

HAIR • NAILS • IMMUNITY BOOSTER • DIGESTION • ENERGY BOOSTER

UNDER 1256 kJ/300 Cal PER SERVE

50 g (1¾ oz/2 cups) kale, stalks removed

50 g (1¾ oz/2 cups) baby spinach

625 ml (21½ fl oz/2½ cups) almond milk

2 frozen bananas

Fresh banana slices, to serve (optional)

Place the kale, baby spinach and milk in a blender and blend until well combined.

Add the frozen bananas and blend again until smooth.

To serve, top with fresh banana slices, if desired.

SERVES 1

PEACHY KEEN

ANTIOXIDANT-RICH • IMMUNITY BOOSTER

DIGESTION • ENERGY BOOSTER

90 g (3¼ oz/2 cups) baby spinach

1 frozen banana

4 peaches, halved and stones removed, plus extra peach slices, to garnish

250 ml (9 fl oz/1 cup) coconut milk

½ teaspoon stevia

Fresh peach slices, to serve (optional)

Place all the ingredients in a blender. Blend to your desired consistency.

Garnish with peach slices and serve.

SERVES 1

BERRY BASH

DETOXIFYING • HAIR • SKIN • NAILS • ANTIOXIDANT-RICH • IMMUNITY BOOSTER
ENERGY BOOSTER • UNDER 1256 kJ/300 Cal PER SERVE

90 g (3¼ oz/2 cups) baby spinach

155 g (5½ oz/1 cup) blueberries

125 ml (4 fl oz/½ cup) pomegranate juice

125 ml (4 fl oz/½ cup) water

Stevia, to taste

Place all the ingredients in a blender. Blend until smooth and enjoy!

SERVES 1

QUICK STICKS

DETOXIFYING • HAIR • SKIN • NAILS • ANTIOXIDANT-RICH • ENERGY BOOSTER

UNDER 1256 kJ/300 Cal PER SERVE

45 g (1½ oz/1 cup) baby spinach

140 g (5 oz/1 cup) mixed berries

250 ml (9 fl oz/1 cup) skim or full-fat milk

Place all the ingredients in a blender. Blend until smooth and enjoy!

SERVES 1

4
fast and fresh

KIWI CRUSH

DETOXIFYING • HAIR • SKIN • NAILS • ANTIOXIDANT-RICH

DIGESTION • ENERGY BOOSTER

90 g (3¼ oz/2 cups) baby spinach

1 frozen banana

2 kiwi fruit, peeled

1 thumb-sized piece fresh ginger
(alternatively you can use ½ teaspoon
ground ginger)

250 ml (9 fl oz/1 cup) coconut milk or
coconut water

250 ml (9 fl oz/1 cup) water

2 cm (¾ in) piece lemon peel

1 teaspoon honey (optional)

Place all the ingredients in a blender and blend until smooth.

SERVES 1

WHITE OUT

HAIR • SKIN • NAILS • ANTIOXIDANT-RICH • IMMUNITY BOOSTER
DIGESTION • ENERGY BOOSTER

5 raw almonds

90 g (3¼ oz/¾ cup) cauliflower florets

1 red apple, cored

1 frozen banana

130 g (4½ oz/½ cup) plain yoghurt

250 ml (9 fl oz/1 cup) almond milk

½ teaspoon ground cinnamon and
extra, to serve

½ teaspoon stevia, or more for added
sweetness

Place the almonds in a blender and blend until finely ground, or you can buy chopped or ground almonds instead.

Add the cauliflower, apple, banana, yoghurt, milk, cinnamon and stevia. Blend until smooth.

Sprinkle with the extra ground cinnamon if desired, and garnish with a cinnamon stick.

SERVES 1

NOTE
Raw cauliflower is fine to use; there's no need to cook it first. Surprisingly, you can't even taste the cauliflower.

THE 3 P.M. PICK-ME-UP

DETOXIFYING • HAIR • SKIN • NAILS • ANTIOXIDANT-RICH • IMMUNITY BOOSTER
DIGESTION • ENERGY BOOSTER

90 g (3¼ oz/2 cups) baby spinach

2 frozen bananas

2 tablespoons coconut oil

4 tablespoons coconut probiotic (available at health food stores)

½ teaspoon maca powder (available at health food stores)

1 scoop vanilla protein powder

500 ml (17 fl oz/2 cups) almond milk

1 teaspoon stevia (optional)

8 ice cubes

2 tablespoons chia seeds

Place all the ingredients, except the chia seeds, in a blender and blend until smooth.

Sprinkle the chia seeds on top.

SERVES 2

TIP
I like to add the flesh of a young coconut if I have one. It just chunks up the smoothie and makes it creamier.

ZING A LING LING

DETOXIFYING • SKIN • ANTIOXIDANT-RICH • IMMUNITY BOOSTER

DIGESTION • ENERGY BOOSTER • UNDER 1256 kJ/300 Cal PER SERVE

25 g (1 oz/1 cup) endive

10 g (¼ oz/½ cup) rocket (arugula)

60 g (2¼ oz/½ cup) raspberries

75 g (2½ oz/½ cup) strawberries, hulled

5 whole radishes, including the leaves

250 ml (9 fl oz/1 cup) coconut milk

250 ml (9 fl oz/1 cup) coconut water

1 teaspoon stevia

Blackberries and extra raspberries, to serve (optional)

Place all the ingredients in a blender and blend until smooth. Top with some extra raspberries and some blackberries if you like.

SERVES 2

TIP

If you want to reduce the peppery taste of the radishes then just add a few more berries.

SPICED OATMEAL & NUTS

HAIR • SKIN • NAILS • ANTIOXIDANT-RICH

DIGESTION • ENERGY BOOSTER

25 g (1 oz/¼ cup) rolled (porridge) oats

60 ml (2 fl oz/¼ cup) water

1 red apple, cored

1 fresh date, pitted

1½ tablespoons almond butter

70 g (2½ oz/¼ cup) plain yoghurt

250 ml (9 fl oz/1 cup) plain milk

Small squeeze of lemon juice

½ teaspoon ground cinnamon

1 teaspoon maple syrup

Pinch of ground turmeric

¼ teaspoon natural vanilla extract

7–8 ice cubes

2 walnuts, to serve

Combine the oats and water, and microwave for 2 minutes. Set aside. (You can also use '90-second oats'. For a portion of this size, I would cook it for 30 seconds.)

Place the apple, date, almond butter, yoghurt, milk, lemon juice, cinnamon, maple syrup, turmeric, vanilla and ice cubes in a blender.

Add the cooked oats and blend until smooth.

To serve, top with the walnuts.

SERVES 1

NOTE
This is pretty much the only smoothie I make without any vegies. I make it when I feel like porridge on the go.

THE WALDORF

DETOXIFYING • HAIR • SKIN • NAILS • ANTIOXIDANT-RICH

IMMUNITY BOOSTER • ENERGY BOOSTER

30 g (1 oz/¼ cup) walnuts

90 g (3¼ oz/2 cups) baby spinach

2 celery stalks

2 small red apples, cored

250 ml (9 fl oz/1 cup) water

125 ml (4 fl oz/½ cup) pomegranate juice

Place the walnuts in a blender and blend until finely ground.

Add the remaining ingredients and blend until smooth.

SERVES 1

YES, PEAS!

DETOXIFYING • SKIN • IMMUNITY BOOSTER

ENERGY BOOSTER

90 g (3¼ oz/2 cups) baby spinach

140 g (5 oz/1 cup) frozen peas

1 frozen banana

½ orange, peeled and seeds removed

2 tablespoons fresh lime juice

250 ml (9 fl oz/1 cup) water

Stevia, to taste

Place all the ingredients in a blender and blend until smooth.

SERVES 1

MAMA TO BE

HAIR • SKIN • NAILS • ANTIOXIDANT-RICH • IMMUNITY BOOSTER
ENERGY BOOSTER

130 g (4½ oz/½ cup) vanilla yoghurt

60 g (2¼ oz/½ cup) cauliflower florets

½ avocado, peeled and stone removed

300 g (10½ oz/2 cups) strawberries, hulled

7 g (¼ oz/¼ cup) basil leaves

1 teaspoon natural vanilla extract

250 ml (9 fl oz/1 cup) skim or full-fat milk

Stevia, to taste (optional)

Place all the ingredients in a blender and blend until smooth.

SERVES 1

NOTE
Cauliflower is perfect for pregnancy diets. It's full of fibre, vitamin C, zinc, folic acid and potassium.

SUMMER IN A JAR

DETOXIFYING • HAIR • SKIN • NAILS • ANTIOXIDANT-RICH • IMMUNITY BOOSTER
DIGESTION • ENERGY BOOSTER • UNDER 1256 kJ/300 Cal PER SERVE

45 g (1½ oz/1 cup) baby spinach

15 g (½ oz/½ cup) kale, stalks removed

30 g (1 oz/½ cup) broccoli florets

1 Lebanese (short) cucumber

1 orange, peeled and seeds removed

1 lemon, peeled and seeds removed

1 frozen banana

Handful of mint leaves

500 ml (17 fl oz/2 cups) water

Place all the ingredients in a blender. Blend until smooth and enjoy!

SERVES 2

THE MOJITO

DETOXIFYING • HAIR • IMMUNITY BOOSTER

DIGESTION • ENERGY BOOSTER

25 g (1 oz/1 cup) kale, stalks removed

1 frozen banana

¼ lime, leave peel on

1 teaspoon natural vanilla extract

10 g (¼ oz/½ cup) mint leaves

250 ml (9 fl oz/1 cup) skim or full-fat milk

Place all the ingredients in a blender and blend until smooth.

SERVES 1

KALE SUNRISE

DETOXIFYING • HAIR • IMMUNITY BOOSTER • DIGESTION
ENERGY BOOSTER

50 g (1¾ oz/2 cups) kale, stalks removed

250 ml (9 fl oz/1 cup) water

1 frozen banana

1½ small oranges, peeled and seeds removed

1 tablespoon chia seeds

Place the kale and water in a blender and blend until well combined.

Add the banana, oranges and chia seeds. Blend again to your desired consistency.

SERVES 1

THE GREEN ROOM

DETOXIFYING • HAIR • SKIN • NAILS

ENERGY BOOSTER

45 g (1½ oz/1 cup) baby spinach

1 Lebanese (short) cucumber

170 g (6 oz/1 cup) chopped honeydew melon

1 tablespoon coconut oil

250 ml (9 fl oz/1 cup) coconut water

Place all the ingredients in a blender. Blend until smooth and enjoy!

SERVES 1

COCONUT ICE

HAIR • SKIN • NAILS • ANTIOXIDANT-RICH

DIGESTION • ENERGY BOOSTER

250 ml (9 fl oz/1 cup) skim or full-fat milk

1 frozen banana

60 g (2¼ oz/½ cup) cauliflower florets

75 g (2½ oz/½ cup) strawberries, hulled

1 tablespoon coconut oil

Stevia, to taste (optional)

Coconut flakes, to serve

Place the milk, banana, cauliflower, strawberries, coconut oil and stevia, if using, in a blender and blend until smooth.

When ready to serve, top with the coconut flakes.

SERVES 1

LYCHEE LOVE

DETOXIFYING • HAIR • ANTIOXIDANT-RICH • IMMUNITY BOOSTER

ENERGY BOOSTER • UNDER 1256 kJ/300 Cal PER SERVE

90 g (3¼ oz/2 cups) baby spinach

9 fresh lychees, peeled (tinned lychees are fine to use if you can't get fresh)

1 frozen banana

10 g (¼ oz/½ cup) mint leaves

250 ml (9 fl oz/1 cup) water

Place all the ingredients in a blender. Blend until smooth and enjoy!

SERVES 1

5
get lean

THE UPLIFTER

DETOXIFYING • ANTIOXIDANT-RICH • DIGESTION • ENERGY BOOSTER

UNDER 1256 kJ/300 Cal PER SERVE

. . . .

180 g (6½ oz/4 cups) baby spinach

160 g (5½ oz/1 cup) chopped pineapple

1 lemon, peeled

1 red grapefruit, peeled

1 cm (½ inch) piece fresh ginger, peeled

500 ml (17 fl oz/2 cups) water

Place all the ingredients in a blender and blend until smooth.

SERVES 1

Super Green Smoothies

WATERMELON DETOX

DETOXIFYING • IMMUNITY BOOSTER • DIGESTION
ENERGY BOOSTER • UNDER 1256 kJ/300 Cal PER SERVE

90 g (3¼ oz/2 cups) baby spinach

375 g (13 oz/2½ cups) chopped seedless watermelon

1 frozen banana

250 ml (9 fl oz/1 cup) water

270 g (9½ oz/2 cups) ice cubes

Place all the ingredients in a blender and blend until smooth.

SERVES 2

NOTE
Don't let the browny-green colour put you off. The watermelon flavour is delicious and refreshing.

FLAT BELLY

HAIR • SKIN • NAILS • ANTIOXIDANT-RICH • IMMUNITY BOOSTER

DIGESTION • ENERGY BOOSTER • UNDER 1256 kJ/300 Cal PER SERVE

45 g (1½ oz/1 cup) baby spinach

¼ avocado, peeled and stone removed

15 g (½ oz/¼ cup) broccoli florets

1 frozen banana

Large handful of mint leaves

3 raw almonds

1 teaspoon coconut oil

250 ml (9 fl oz/1 cup) almond milk

1 teaspoon stevia, to taste

Place all the ingredients in a blender and blend until smooth.

SERVES 1

ROCKET FUEL

HAIR • SKIN • NAILS • ANTIOXIDANT-RICH • DIGESTION
ENERGY BOOSTER • UNDER 1256 kJ/300 Cal PER SERVE

20 g (¾ oz/1 cup) rocket (arugula)

90 g (3¼ oz/2 cups) baby spinach

2 pears, cored

1 frozen banana

1 teaspoon chlorophyll liquid (available at
health food stores)

500 ml (17 fl oz/2 cups) soy milk or almond
milk

1 tablespoon honey (optional)

Place all the ingredients in
a blender and blend until
smooth.

SERVES 2

SWEET & SKINNY

DETOXIFYING • SKIN • ANTIOXIDANT-RICH • IMMUNITY BOOSTER • DIGESTION

ENERGY BOOSTER • UNDER 1256 kJ/300 Cal PER SERVE

375 g (13 oz/3 cups) cauliflower florets

280 g (10 oz/1½ cups) chopped mango

160 g (5½ oz/1 cup) chopped pineapple

500 ml (17 fl oz/2 cups) almond milk or rice milk

1 tablespoon coconut oil

70 g (2½ oz/½ cup) ice cubes

Place the cauliflower, mango, pineapple and milk in a blender and blend until well combined.

Add the coconut oil and ice cubes, and blend until smooth.

Serve in a tall glass and enjoy!

SERVES 2

NOTE

To turn this into a green smoothie, add 90 g (3¼ oz/2 cups) of baby spinach.

ESPRESSO YOURSELF

ANTIOXIDANT-RICH • DIGESTION • ENERGY BOOSTER

UNDER 1256 kJ/300 Cal PER SERVE

45 g (1½ oz/1 cup) baby spinach

1 frozen banana

1 tablespoon espresso

250 ml (9 fl oz/1 cup) almond milk

250 ml (9 fl oz/1 cup) water

Handful of ice cubes

½ teaspoon stevia

Place all the ingredients in a blender and blend until smooth.

SERVES 1

NOTE

Midweek, when I'm in a rush, I use a capsule-based espresso machine to pour a short black. Weekends, I grind my own beans and make an espresso using a proper coffee machine. If instant is your thing, that's totally OK too.

ENERGY BOOSTER

HAIR • SKIN • NAILS • ANTIOXIDANT-RICH • DIGESTION
ENERGY BOOSTER • UNDER 1256 kJ/300 Cal PER SERVE

90 g (3¼ oz/2 cups) baby spinach

30 g (1 oz/½ cup) broccoli florets

7 g (⅛ oz/¼ cup) endive

1 frozen banana

½ frozen mango

2 tablespoons chia seeds

2 tablespoons goji berries

1 scoop vanilla protein powder

750 ml (26 fl oz/3 cups) water

Soak the goji berries in water for 15 minutes so they blend easily. Drain the goji berries and place them in a blender with the remaining ingredients and blend until smooth.

SERVES 2

ORANGE COUNTY

DETOXIFYING • ANTIOXIDANT-RICH • IMMUNITY BOOSTER • DIGESTION
ENERGY BOOSTER • UNDER 1256 kJ/300 Cal PER SERVE

90 g (3¼ oz/2 cups) baby spinach

1 large silverbeet (Swiss chard) leaf, stem removed

3 small brussels sprouts

1 frozen banana

2 frozen oranges, peeled

2 tablespoons agave syrup or honey

250 ml (9 fl oz/1 cup) water

7–8 ice cubes if you're not using frozen oranges

Place all the ingredients in a blender and blend until smooth.

SERVES 2

MELONADE

DETOXIFYING • HAIR • SKIN • NAILS • ANTIOXIDANT-RICH • IMMUNITY BOOSTER
ENERGY BOOSTER • UNDER 1256 kJ/300 Cal PER SERVE

90 g (3¼ oz/2 cups) baby spinach

5 g (⅛ oz/¼ cup) mint leaves, or to taste

125 ml (4 fl oz/½ cup) water

170 g (6 oz/1 cup) chopped honeydew melon

1 pear, cored

½ lemon, peeled and seeds removed

Place the baby spinach, mint and water in a blender and blend until well combined.

Add the remaining ingredients and blend again until smooth.

SERVES 1

THE FAT FLUSH

DETOXIFYING • ANTIOXIDANT-RICH • IMMUNITY BOOSTER • DIGESTION

ENERGY BOOSTER • UNDER 1256 kJ/300 Cal PER SERVE

45 g (1½ oz/1 cup) baby spinach

½ avocado, peeled and stone removed

1 Lebanese (short) cucumber

340 g (12 oz/2 cups) chopped honeydew melon

1 frozen banana

500 ml (17 fl oz/2 cups) almond milk

Place all the ingredients in a blender and blend until smooth. Enjoy!

SERVES 2

LIVER CLEANSER

DETOXIFYING • ANTIOXIDANT-RICH • IMMUNITY BOOSTER • DIGESTION
ENERGY BOOSTER • UNDER 1256 kJ/300 Cal PER SERVE

45 g (1½ oz/1 cup) baby spinach

1½ beetroot (beets), peeled and chopped

15 g (½ oz/½ cup) kale, stalks removed

1 small apple, cored

1 orange, peeled

Handful of frozen mixed berries

80 g (2¾ oz/½ cup) frozen pineapple pieces (optional)

250 ml (9 fl oz/1 cup) water

135 g (4¾ oz/1 cup) ice cubes

Place all the ingredients in a blender and blend until smooth.

SERVES 2

Super Green Smoothies

SKIN GLOW

DETOXIFYING • SKIN • IMMUNITY BOOSTER • ENERGY BOOSTER

UNDER 1256 kJ/300 Cal PER SERVE

90 g (3¼ oz/2 cups) baby spinach

15 g (½ oz/¼ cup) alfalfa sprouts

180 g (6½ oz/1 cup) red grapes

2 kiwi fruit, peeled

250 ml (9 fl oz/1 cup) almond milk

6 ice cubes

Place all the ingredients in a blender and blend until smooth.

SERVES 1

ULTIMATE POWER

HAIR • SKIN • NAILS • ANTIOXIDANT-RICH • IMMUNITY BOOSTER • DIGESTION
ENERGY BOOSTER • UNDER 1256 kJ/300 Cal PER SERVE

25 g (1 oz/½ cup) baby spinach

1 avocado, halved and stone removed

1 Lebanese (short) cucumber

15 g (½ oz/½ cup) bok choy (pak choy)

15 g (½ oz/½ cup) radicchio

10 g (¼ oz/½ cup) rocket (arugula)

2 frozen bananas

500 ml (17 fl oz/2 cups) water

1 teaspoon stevia

Seeds from ¼ pomegranate for garnish

Place all the ingredients, except the pomegranate seeds, in a blender and blend until smooth.

Top with the pomegranate seeds.

SERVES 2

PAPAYA PUMPKIN

DETOXIFYING • HAIR • SKIN • NAILS • ANTIOXIDANT-RICH • DIGESTION
ENERGY BOOSTER • UNDER 1256 kJ/300 Cal PER SERVE

150 g (5½ oz/1 cup) chopped pumpkin (winter squash)

25 g (1 oz/½ cup) baby spinach

185 g (6½ oz/1 cup) chopped papaya

1 teaspoon vanilla protein powder

500 ml (17 fl oz/2 cups) vanilla almond milk

½ teaspoon allspice

½ teaspoon ground ginger

½ teaspoon freshly grated nutmeg

Pinch of ground cinnamon

1 teaspoon stevia, or more to taste

Handful of ice cubes

Place all the ingredients in a blender and blend until smooth.

SERVES 1

NOTE
If you have time, you can steam the pumpkin and let it cool. The cooking brings out the sweetness in the pumpkin. If you haven't planned ahead you can use raw pumpkin. It still has all the health benefits but the recipe might need a bit more sweetener.

THE ORIGINAL SKINNY

DETOXIFYING • HAIR • SKIN • NAILS • ANTIOXIDANT-RICH • IMMUNITY BOOSTER

DIGESTION • ENERGY BOOSTER • UNDER 1256 kJ/300 Cal PER SERVE

1 avocado, halved, peeled and stone removed

60 g (2¼ oz/1 cup) broccoli florets

25 g (1 oz/1 cup) kale, stalks removed

45 g (1½ oz/1 cup) baby spinach

2 celery stalks

1 frozen banana

2 passionfruit

Large handful of mint leaves

1 teaspoon chia seeds

1 tablespoon cleansing fibre powder (available at health food stores)

Juice of 1 lemon

70 g (2½ oz/½ cup) ice cubes

500 ml (17 fl oz/2 cups) water

1 teaspoon stevia

Place all the ingredients in a blender. Blend for a couple of minutes until the desired consistency is reached. I like mine smooth and creamy.

SERVES 2

NOTE

The blended passionfruit seeds make the smoothie a bit gritty. If that doesn't appeal to you, stir the passionfruit seeds into the smoothie after the other ingredients have been blended.

This is the first smoothie I started making, so naturally I have a bit of a soft spot for it. It's green and it's full of vegetables with a bit of fruit for sweetness. I feel amazing every time I drink this.

BIKINI BABE

DETOXIFYING • SKIN • ANTIOXIDANT-RICH • IMMUNITY BOOSTER

ENERGY BOOSTER • UNDER 1256 kJ/300 Cal PER SERVE

90 g (3¼ oz/2 cups) baby spinach

25 g (1 oz/1 cup) kale, stalks removed

7 g (¼ oz/¼ cup) watercress

500 ml (17 fl oz/2 cups) almond milk

30 g (1 oz/½ cup) broccoli florets

¼ avocado, peeled and stone removed

185 g (6½ oz/1 cup) chopped mango

1 tablespoon chia seeds

2 teaspoons green supplement powder
(available at health food stores)

Place the baby spinach, kale and watercress in a blender with the almond milk and blend until well combined.

Add the remaining ingredients and blend until smooth.

SERVES 2

SMOOTHIE ME SKINNY

DETOXIFYING • HAIR • SKIN • NAILS • ANTIOXIDANT-RICH • IMMUNITY BOOSTER
DIGESTION • ENERGY BOOSTER • UNDER 1256 kJ/300 Cal PER SERVE

45 g (1½ oz/1 cup) baby spinach

1 Lebanese (short) cucumber

30 g (1 oz/½ cup) broccoli florets

1 lime, peeled and seeds removed

160 g (5½ oz/1 cup) chopped pineapple

250 ml (9 fl oz/1 cup) water

Place all the ingredients in a blender and blend until smooth.

SERVES 1

KIWI KICKER

DETOXIFYING • HAIR • SKIN • NAILS • ANTIOXIDANT-RICH • IMMUNITY BOOSTER
ENERGY BOOSTER • UNDER 1256 kJ/300 Cal PER SERVE

45 g (1½ oz/1 cup) baby spinach

30 g (1 oz/½ cup) broccoli florets

2 kiwi fruit, peeled

95 g (3¼ oz/½ cup) chopped mango

2 tablespoons chia seeds

500 ml (17 fl oz/2 cups) water

Place all the ingredients in a blender and blend until smooth.

SERVES 1

KICK-START CLEANSER

DETOXIFYING • HAIR • NAILS • IMMUNITY BOOSTER • DIGESTION
ENERGY BOOSTER • UNDER 1256 kJ/300 Cal PER SERVE

45 g (1½ oz/1 cup) baby spinach

2 tomatoes

1 celery stalk

1 carrot

185 g (6½ oz/1 cup) chopped mango

250 ml (9 fl oz/1 cup) water

Place all the ingredients in a blender and blend until smooth.

SERVES 1

ALL HAIL KING KALE

DETOXIFYING • SKIN • ANTIOXIDANT-RICH • IMMUNITY BOOSTER
DIGESTION • ENERGY BOOSTER • UNDER 1256 kJ/300 Cal PER SERVE

90 g (3¼ oz/2 cups) baby spinach

25 g (1 oz/1 cup) kale, stalks removed

45 g (1½ oz/¼ cup) green grapes

2 passionfruit

185 g (6½ oz/1 cup) paw paw or papaya

Handful of flat-leaf (Italian) parsley, stems removed

1 tablespoon probiotic powder (available at health food stores)

500 ml (17 fl oz/2 cups) water

Sweetener (stevia, agave or rice malt syrup) (optional)

Place all the ingredients in a blender and blend until smooth.

Add a sweetener to taste.

SERVES 2

NOTE
The blended passionfruit seeds make the smoothie a bit gritty. If that doesn't appeal to you, stir the passionfruit seeds into the smoothie after the other ingredients have been blended.

6
all vegies

GREEN MARY

DETOXIFYING • SKIN • IMMUNITY BOOSTER • DIGESTION • ENERGY BOOSTER

UNDER 1256 kJ/300 Cal PER SERVE

10 ice cubes

90 g (3¼ oz/2 cups) baby spinach

1 celery stalk

1 Lebanese (short) cucumber

2 small tomatoes

½ small red capsicum (pepper)

Small handful of flat-leaf (Italian) parsley (optional)

1 shallot, peeled

½ teaspoon Tabasco sauce or cayenne pepper

2 generous pinches of salt

Black pepper, to taste

185 ml (6 fl oz/¾ cup) water

Place the ice cubes in a blender. Add the remaining ingredients and blend until smooth.

SERVES 2

TIGHTER TUMMY

DETOXIFYING • IMMUNITY BOOSTER • DIGESTION • ENERGY BOOSTER

UNDER 1256 kJ/300 Cal PER SERVE

45 g (1½ oz/1 cup) baby spinach

1 Lebanese (short) cucumber

1 lemon, peeled and seeds removed

2 cm (¾ inch) piece fresh ginger, peeled (use less or more, to taste)

5 g (⅛ oz/¼ cup) mint leaves

500 ml (17 fl oz/2 cups) water

Place all the ingredients in a blender and blend until smooth.

SERVES 1

CITRUS ZINGER

DETOXIFYING • HAIR • SKIN • NAILS • IMMUNITY BOOSTER

DIGESTION • ENERGY BOOSTER

45 g (1½ oz/1 cup) baby spinach

25 g (1 oz/1 cup) kale, stalks removed

Large handful of mint leaves

375 ml (13 fl oz/1½ cups) water

1 Lebanese (short) cucumber

1 tablespoon coconut oil

1 lemon, peeled and seeds removed

1 lime, peeled and seeds removed

Handful of ice cubes

Stevia, to taste (optional)

Place the baby spinach, kale, mint leaves and water in a blender and blend until smooth.

Add the remaining ingredients and blend until it reaches your desired consistency.

SERVES 1

Super Green Smoothies

PARSLEY PUNCH

DETOXIFYING • HAIR • SKIN • NAILS • IMMUNITY BOOSTER

DIGESTION • ENERGY BOOSTER

90 g (3¼ oz/2 cups) baby spinach

1 Lebanese (short) cucumber

½ avocado, peeled and stone removed

10 g (¼ oz/½ cup) flat-leaf (Italian) parsley

1 lemon, peeled and seeds removed

375 ml (13 fl oz/1½ cups) coconut water

70 g (2½ oz/½ cup) ice cubes

Place all the ingredients in a blender and blend to your desired consistency.

SERVES 1

TIP

Add a little more coconut water if the consistency is too thick.

THE BIG DAY

DETOXIFYING • HAIR • SKIN • NAILS • ANTIOXIDANT-RICH • IMMUNITY BOOSTER

DIGESTION • ENERGY BOOSTER • UNDER 1256 kJ/300 Cal

45 g (1½ oz/1 cup) baby spinach

25 g (1 oz/1 cup) kale, stalks removed

500 ml (17 fl oz/2 cups) water

Handful of ice cubes

30 g (1 oz/½ cup) broccoli florets

1 Lebanese (short) cucumber

1 celery stalk

2 cm (¾ inch) piece fresh ginger, peeled

1 lemon, peeled and seeds removed

¼ lime, peeled and seeds removed

Stevia, to taste

Place the baby spinach, kale, water and ice cubes in a blender and blend for 30 seconds.

Add the remaining ingredients and blend until smooth.

SERVES 2

NOTE

This smoothie is named in honour of all those big events—weddings, parties, even the bikini season—that we want to feel our best for. At less than a quarter of one kilojoule (54 calories), it is a fast, energy-filled road to lean. Happy big day!

Super Green Smoothies

7

something
sweet

COCO-PINE

HAIR • SKIN • NAILS • ANTIOXIDANT-RICH

IMMUNITY BOOSTER • ENERGY BOOSTER

1 tablespoon coconut flakes

185 g (6½ oz/1½ cups) cauliflower florets

1 frozen banana

160 g (5½ oz/1 cup) frozen pineapple pieces

70 g (2½ oz/¼ cup) plain or coconut yoghurt

250 ml (9 fl oz/1 cup) coconut milk

1 teaspoon stevia

Place the coconut flakes in a small frying pan over medium–low heat, then stir constantly until golden brown. Remove from the heat. Set aside to cool. (Be careful as coconut flakes cook quite quickly and they can burn easily.)

Place the cauliflower, banana, pineapple, yoghurt, coconut milk and stevia in a blender. Blend until smooth.

Pour into a big tall glass and top with the toasted coconut flakes. Serve immediately.

SERVES 1

HOLY CACAO!

SKIN • ANTIOXIDANT-RICH • IMMUNITY BOOSTER • DIGESTION
ENERGY BOOSTER • UNDER 1256 kJ/300 Cal PER SERVE

185 g (6½ oz/1½ cups) cauliflower florets

25 g (1 oz/½ cup) baby spinach

½ avocado, peeled and stone removed

5 fresh dates, pitted

1 teaspoon cacao powder

1 scoop chocolate protein powder

750 ml (26 fl oz/3 cups) vanilla or plain
almond milk

135 g (4¾ oz/1 cup) ice cubes

Additional sweetener (stevia, agave or
rice malt syrup), to taste (optional)

Place all the ingredients in a blender and blend until completely smooth and creamy.

SERVES 2

TIP

If you don't want a thick smoothie like this, just drop the avocado and add a touch more milk.

CHOC-MINT

DETOXIFYING • ANTIOXIDANT-RICH

DIGESTION • ENERGY BOOSTER

2 peppermint tea bags

250 ml (9 fl oz/1 cup) boiling water

90 g (3¼ oz/2 cups) baby spinach

1 frozen banana

Handful of mint leaves

2 tablespoons coconut oil

2 scoops chocolate protein powder

250 ml (9 fl oz/1 cup) oat milk

1 teaspoon cacao powder

6–7 ice cubes

2 teaspoons stevia

Steep the tea bags in the boiling water so that it's concentrated. Wait about 30 minutes or until the water has cooled. I usually make my tea at night and leave it in the fridge until morning. If you're in a rush, pop it in the freezer.

Place the peppermint tea and remaining ingredients in a blender. Blend until smooth.

SERVES 2

BERRY ELIXIR

SKIN • ANTIOXIDANT-RICH • IMMUNITY BOOSTER

DIGESTION • ENERGY BOOSTER

2 heaped tablespoons goji berries

45 g (1½ oz/1 cup) baby spinach

155 g (5½ oz/1 cup) blueberries

125 g (4½ oz/1 cup) raspberries

2 fresh dates, pitted

5 walnuts

1 tablespoon cold-pressed
flaxseed (linseed) oil

250 ml (9 fl oz/1 cup) water

Soak the goji berries in water for 15 minutes so they blend easily. Drain the berries and place them in a blender with the remaining ingredients. Blend until smooth and creamy.

SERVES 1

TIP

If you freeze this smoothie it turns into a delicious granita. Highly recommended!

THE PBC

HAIR • SKIN • NAILS • ANTIOXIDANT-RICH

ENERGY BOOSTER

270 g (9½ oz/2 cups) ice cubes

500 ml (17 fl oz/2 cups) almond milk

135 g (4¾ oz/3 cups) baby spinach

½ large avocado, peeled and stone removed

1 large frozen banana

6 large fresh dates, pitted

2 tablespoons peanut butter

3 tablespoons cocoa powder

Whipped cream, to serve (optional)

Place the ice cubes in a blender.

Pour in the almond milk then add the baby spinach, avocado, banana, dates, peanut butter and cocoa powder. Blend until smooth.

Obviously, the cream is an optional extra!

SERVES 2

NOTE
This peanut butter and chocolate smoothie is an awesome dessert substitute. It's a major chocolate hit.

PUMPKIN PIE

DETOXIFYING • HAIR • IMMUNITY BOOSTER • DIGESTION

ENERGY BOOSTER • UNDER 1256 kJ/300 Cal PER SERVE

90 g (3¼ oz/2 cups) baby spinach

155 g (5½ oz/1 cup) finely chopped
pumpkin (raw is fine)

2 frozen bananas

4 fresh dates, pitted

1 teaspoon natural vanilla extract

¼ teaspoon freshly grated nutmeg

½ teaspoon ground cinnamon

¼ teaspoon allspice

500 ml (17 fl oz/2 cups) almond milk

Place all the ingredients in a blender. Blend until smooth and enjoy!

SERVES 2

CHOC CHERRY

DETOXIFYING • HAIR • SKIN • NAILS

ANTIOXIDANT-RICH • ENERGY BOOSTER

70 g (2½ oz/1½ cups) baby spinach

1 frozen banana

130 g (4½ oz/½ cup) Greek yoghurt

150 g (5½ oz/1 cup) pitted cherries

1 tablespoon cacao powder

1 teaspoon natural vanilla extract

250 ml (9 fl oz/1 cup) skim or full-fat milk

Extra pitted cherries and cacao nibs,
to serve (optional)

Place all the ingredients in a blender. Blend until smooth.

If you like, top with extra cherries and cacao nibs and enjoy!

SERVES 1

APPLE PIE

DETOXIFYING • HAIR • SKIN • NAILS
DIGESTION • ENERGY BOOSTER

25 g (1 oz/1 cup) kale, stalks removed

¼ avocado, peeled and stone removed

1 granny smith apple, cored

1 frozen banana

1 tablespoon almond butter

1 teaspoon ground cinnamon

250 ml (9 fl oz/1 cup) skim or full-fat milk

250 ml (9 fl oz/1 cup) water

Place all the ingredients in a blender and blend until smooth.

SERVES 1

VANILLA KEY LIME

DETOXIFYING • HAIR • IMMUNITY BOOSTER

DIGESTION • ENERGY BOOSTER

70 g (2½ oz/1½ cups) baby spinach

130 g (4½ oz/½ cup) vanilla yoghurt

1 frozen banana

2 tablespoons fresh lime juice

½ teaspoon natural vanilla extract

250 ml (9 fl oz/1 cup) skim or full-fat milk

Place all the ingredients in a blender and blend until smooth.

SERVES 1

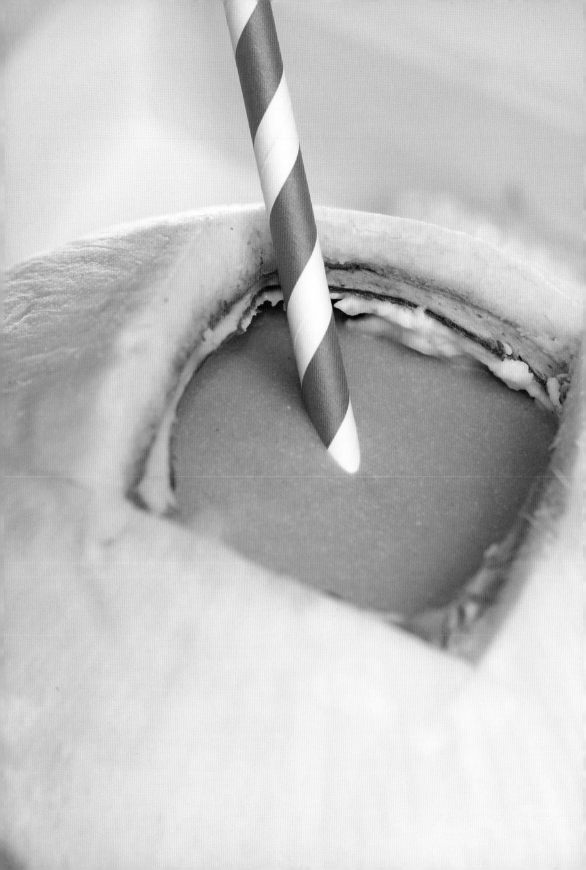

CALIFORNIA DREAMING

DETOXIFYING • HAIR • SKIN • NAILS • ANTIOXIDANT-RICH

IMMUNITY BOOSTER • DIGESTION • ENERGY BOOSTER

75 g (2½ oz/3 cups) kale, stalks removed

250 ml (9 fl oz/1 cup) unsweetened coconut milk

½ lime, peeled and seeds removed

1 mango, peeled, halved and stone removed

½ frozen banana

Place the kale and coconut milk in a blender and blend until well combined.

Add the lime, mango and banana and blend until smooth.

SERVES 1

8
kid-friendly

GREEÑ-A COLADA

DETOXIFYING • ANTIOXIDANT-RICH • IMMUNITY BOOSTER

DIGESTION • ENERGY BOOSTER

135 g (4¾ oz/3 cups) baby spinach

320 g (11¼ oz/2 cups) chopped pineapple
(ideally fresh, though tinned pineapple
drained of its juice is fine)

1 frozen banana

Large handful of mint leaves

250 ml (9 fl oz/1 cup) coconut water

250 ml (9 fl oz/1 cup) coconut milk

Place the baby spinach, pineapple, banana and mint in a blender, add the coconut water and coconut milk and blend until smooth.

SERVES 2

NOTE
If you're trying to get more greens into your kids, then this is a great one to start with.

PURPLE POWER

DETOXIFYING • HAIR • SKIN • NAILS

ANTIOXIDANT-RICH • ENERGY BOOSTER

25 g (1 oz/½ cup) baby spinach

1 apple, cored

155 g (5½ oz/1 cup) blueberries

130 g (4½ oz/½ cup) vanilla yoghurt

125 ml (4 fl oz/½ cup) skim or full-fat milk

2 teaspoons honey (optional)

Place all the ingredients in a blender and blend until smooth.

Add the honey to sweeten it a little more if you like.

SERVES 1

Kid-friendly

CHERRY BERRY JAM

DETOXIFYING • HAIR • SKIN • NAILS

ANTIOXIDANT-RICH • DIGESTION • ENERGY BOOSTER

150 g (5½ oz/1 cup) pitted cherries

125 g (4½ oz/1 cup) raspberries

90 g (3¼ oz/2 cups) baby spinach

½ frozen banana

375 ml (13 fl oz/1½ cups) skim
or full-fat milk

Place all the ingredients in a blender and blend until smooth. Enjoy!

SERVES 1

STRAWBERRY SHORTCAKE

HAIR • SKIN • NAILS • ANTIOXIDANT-RICH

IMMUNITY BOOSTER • ENERGY BOOSTER

45 g (1½ oz/1 cup) baby spinach

300 g (10½ oz/2 cups) strawberries, hulled

130 g (4½ oz/½ cup) vanilla yoghurt

2 teaspoons rice malt syrup
(for sweetness)

375 ml (13 fl oz/1½ cups) skim
or full-fat milk

Place all the ingredients in a blender and blend until smooth.

SERVES 1

PIECE OF CAKE

DETOXIFYING • HAIR • NAILS

DIGESTION • ENERGY BOOSTER

90 g (3¼ oz/2 cups) baby spinach

1 frozen banana

4 fresh dates, pitted

1 teaspoon natural vanilla extract

375 ml (13 fl oz/1½ cups) skim
or full-fat milk

70 g (2½ oz/½ cup) ice cubes

Place all the ingredients in a blender. Blend until smooth and enjoy!

SERVES 1

GREEN MACHINE

DETOXIFYING • HAIR • SKIN • NAILS • DIGESTION • ENERGY BOOSTER

UNDER 1256 kJ/300 Cal PER SERVE

90 g (3¼ oz/2 cups) baby spinach

¼ avocado, peeled and stone removed

1 pear, cored

250 ml (9 fl oz/1 cup) coconut water

250 ml (9 fl oz/1 cup) water

Stevia, to taste (optional)

Place all the ingredients in a blender and blend until smooth.

SERVES 2

Kid-friendly

your guide to the benefits

smoothie	benefits								
	DETOXIFYING	HAIR	SKIN	NAILS	ANTIOXIDANT-RICH	IMMUNITY BOOSTER	DIGESTION	UNDER 1256 kJ/ 300 Cal PER SERVE	ENERGY BOOSTER
All Hail King Kale	✓		✓		✓	✓	✓	✓	✓
Apple Pie	✓	✓	✓	✓			✓		✓
Bananarama		✓		✓		✓	✓	✓	✓
Berry Bash	✓	✓	✓	✓	✓	✓		✓	✓
Berry Elixir			✓		✓	✓	✓		✓
Bikini Babe	✓		✓		✓	✓		✓	✓
California Dreaming	✓	✓	✓	✓	✓	✓	✓		
Cherry Berry Jam	✓	✓	✓	✓	✓		✓		✓
Choc Cherry	✓	✓	✓	✓	✓				✓
Choc-Mint	✓				✓				✓
Citrus Zinger	✓	✓	✓	✓		✓	✓		✓
Coco-Pine		✓	✓	✓	✓	✓			✓
Coconut Ice		✓	✓	✓	✓		✓		✓
Energy Booster		✓	✓	✓	✓		✓	✓	✓
Espresso Yourself					✓		✓	✓	✓
Flat Belly		✓	✓	✓	✓	✓		✓	✓
Green Machine	✓	✓	✓	✓			✓	✓	✓
Green Mary	✓		✓			✓	✓	✓	✓
Greeñ-a Colada	✓				✓	✓	✓		✓
Holy Cacao!			✓		✓	✓	✓	✓	
Kale Sunrise	✓	✓				✓	✓		✓
Kick-start Cleanser	✓	✓		✓		✓	✓	✓	✓
Kiwi Crush	✓	✓	✓	✓	✓				✓
Kiwi Kicker	✓	✓	✓	✓	✓	✓		✓	✓
Liver Cleanser	✓				✓	✓	✓	✓	✓
Lychee Love	✓	✓			✓	✓		✓	✓
Mama To Be		✓	✓	✓	✓	✓			✓
Mango Magic	✓	✓	✓	✓	✓		✓	✓	✓
Melonade	✓	✓	✓	✓	✓	✓			✓
Orange County	✓				✓	✓	✓	✓	✓

smoothie	benefits								
	DETOXIFYING	HAIR	SKIN	NAILS	ANTIOXIDANT-RICH	IMMUNITY BOOSTER	DIGESTION	UNDER 1256 kJ/ 300 Cal PER SERVE	ENERGY BOOSTER
Papaya Pumpkin	✓	✓	✓	✓	✓		✓	✓	✓
Parsley Punch	✓	✓	✓	✓		✓	✓		✓
Peachy Keen					✓	✓	✓		✓
Piece of Cake	✓	✓		✓			✓		✓
Pumpkin Pie	✓	✓				✓	✓	✓	✓
Purple Power	✓	✓	✓	✓	✓				✓
Quick Sticks	✓	✓	✓	✓	✓			✓	✓
Rocket Fuel		✓	✓	✓	✓		✓	✓	✓
Skin Glow	✓		✓			✓		✓	✓
Smoothie Me Skinny	✓	✓	✓	✓		✓	✓	✓	✓
Spiced Oatmeal & Nuts		✓	✓	✓	✓		✓		✓
Strawberry Shortcake		✓	✓	✓	✓	✓			✓
Summer in a Jar	✓	✓	✓	✓	✓	✓	✓	✓	✓
Sweet & Skinny	✓		✓		✓	✓	✓	✓	✓
The 3 p.m. Pick-Me-Up	✓	✓	✓	✓	✓	✓	✓		✓
The Big Day	✓	✓	✓	✓	✓	✓		✓	✓
The Fat Flush	✓				✓	✓	✓	✓	✓
The Green Room	✓	✓	✓	✓					✓
The Mojito	✓	✓				✓	✓		✓
The Original Skinny	✓	✓	✓	✓	✓	✓	✓	✓	✓
The PBC		✓	✓	✓	✓				✓
The Uplifter	✓				✓		✓	✓	✓
The Waldorf	✓	✓	✓	✓	✓	✓			✓
Tighter Tummy	✓					✓	✓	✓	✓
Ultimate Power		✓	✓	✓	✓	✓	✓	✓	✓
Vanilla Key Lime	✓	✓				✓	✓		✓
Watermelon Detox	✓					✓	✓	✓	✓
White Out		✓	✓	✓	✓		✓		✓
Yes, Peas!	✓		✓			✓			✓
Zing a Ling Ling	✓		✓		✓	✓	✓	✓	✓

index

photography credits

Peter Brew-Bevan
Pages ii, x, xiv–1, 2, 4, 16 and 174.

Jason Hinsch
Pages 6, 8, 11, 12, 28–9, 32, 35, 36, 46, 49, 50, 53,
77, 81, 83, 87, 88, 91, 95, 96, 99, 100, 102, 105,
114, 133, 134, 137, 138, 155 and 178.

Maha Koraiem
Pages 78, 84 and 141.

Andy Miao
Pages vi–vii, viii, xiii, 14, 20, 25, 26–7, 30, 39,
40, 42, 45, 54, 57, 58, 61, 62, 65, 66, 69, 70, 72–3,
74, 92, 106, 109, 110, 113, 116–17, 118, 121, 122,
125, 126, 129, 130, 142, 145, 146, 149, 150, 152,
156, 159, 160, 163, 164, 168–9, 172 and 173.

thank you

This book would not have been possible without the support and help of these people we are fortunate enough to have in our lives …

Peter Brew-Bevan: It is always a joy to work with you. Here's to many more shoots and many more books.

Jason Hinsch: I know you'll never be able to look at spinach the same way again. Thank you for not only such beautiful shots but also for laughing with us all the way through it. Nothing has changed in all these years.

Andy Miao: Like legit, you are awesome. We are so proud of you and hopefully one day when you are rich and famous you will remember us. YOLO.

Sara Williams: Sars, we couldn't have done it without you. Thank you for being across everything, thinking ahead, covering our arses and keeping us sane and fed. We love you.

Our team at swiish.com.au, past and present, you know who you are: We thank you all for throwing yourselves into this wholeheartedly. An extra big shout out to Shaza, Natasha, Michaela and Renee for going the extra mile and putting up with our endless new ideas!

Clare Smith, David Dalton, Claire Kingston: Thank you for believing in this book as much as we do, and for your commitment, passion, drive and dedication.

Our mum and dad: Hi, Mum and Dad!! How lucky that you are a glass jar collector, Mum! Hahaha. Who knew that empty Vegemite, Nescafé and gherkin jars would come in handy??!! Thanks for all your love and support. We love you.

James and Christiane Duigan: Your goodness and kindness radiate from the inside out. Thank you for your kind words about our book. Your love and support is so deeply appreciated.

Shannon Killeen and Monika Bunic: Thank you for making us look so good. Love you guys.

still want more?

No worries ... we've got lots more!

We'd love for you to check in with us at our website, **www.swiish.com.au**, and subscribe for new recipes, videos, tips, tricks, giveaways and lots more. We upload new recipes to Sal's Kitchen regularly.

You can also find us:

On Instagram **@swiishbysallyo**

On Twitter at **twitter.com/swiishbysallyo**

On Facebook at **facebook.com/swiishbysallyobermeder**

Don't forget to tag SWIISH in your snaps, selfies, healthies (healthy selfies!) and share with us your favourite green smoothie recipe, so that we can share it with all the other Super Green Smoothies fans.

Connect with Sally Obermeder:

On Instagram **@sallyobermeder**

On Twitter at **twitter.com/sallyobermeder**

On Facebook at **facebook.com/sallyobermeder**

Connect with Maha Koraiem:

On Instagram **@maha_koraiem**

On Twitter at **twitter.com/maha_koraiem**

On Facebook at **facebook.com/maha.koraiem**

Sally's journey through work, life, near death and back to 'fabulous' is as uplifting as it is inspiring.

Larry Emdur

Heartache, hope and some very high heels

Never Stop *Believing*

SALLY OBERMEDER

Now available in bookshops
and also online as an ebook

about Sally

Sally Obermeder is the founder of the lifestyle website, swiish.com.au. With an obsession for all things luxe for less, Sally's expert eye for what's fabulous and affordable has made SWIISH the go-to site where women get their fix of fashion, beauty, health and home.

SWIISH is all about the quickest, easiest and most affordable ways to look chic and feel great. Everything on SWIISH is covered with Sally's trademark style, strength, positivity and humour.

Sally also includes a behind-the-scenes look at her life on TV, and on and off the red carpet—the happy bits, the glam parts and the tough times too.

After a public battle with aggressive breast cancer, Sally has come back with even more passion for life. She is the co-host of Australia's Channel 7 national news and lifestyle show, *The Daily Edition*, as well as the author of her bestselling memoir, *Never Stop Believing* (Allen & Unwin, 2013).

Sally has always been committed to healthy living. As a qualified personal trainer and Pilates instructor, Sally knows that good health is everything, and everything begins with good health. Ultimately she stands by living a life of balance and happiness … and Sally is proof that balance not only means a daily green smoothie but also that you can have your cake and eat it too—her favourite is tiramisu (just don't eat the whole cake!).